Self Publishing

Step-by-Step

How to Publish Your Book Using Amazon and Other Platforms

Table of Contents

INTRODUCTION

CHAPTER 1: WHY SELF-PUBLISH

CHAPTER 2: BEFORE YOU BEGIN WRITING

CHAPTER 3: TO MARKET, TO MARKET

CHAPTER 4: KINDLE PUBLISHING

CHAPTER 5: SELF PUBLISH YOUR BOOK WITH AMAZON'S CREATESPACE

CHAPTER 6: HOW TO PUBLISH A BOOK

CHAPTER 7: 10 SIMPLE STEPS TO SELF-PUBLISH

CHAPTER 8: PRINT ON DEMAND BOOKS

CHAPTER 9: Bonus Chapter for Making More Money at No Added Cost, Life is Sweet!

CONCLUSION

INTRODUCTION

Self-publishing is an attractive and inexpensive way to get your book out there Self-publishing is the publishing of books and other media by the authors of those works, rather than by established, third-party publishers. Although it represents a small percentage of the publishing industry in terms of sales; it has been present in one form or another since the beginning of publishing and has seen an increase in activity with the advancement of publishing technology, including xerography, desktop publishing systems, print on demand, and the World Wide Web. Cultural phenomena such as the punk/DIY movement, the proliferation of media channels, and blogging have contributed to the advancement of self-publishing.

The key distinguishing characteristic of self-publishing is the absence of a traditional publisher. Instead, the creator or creators, fulfill this role, taking editorial control of the content, arranging for printing, marketing the material, and often distributing it, either directly to consumers or to retailers. Less often, the author prints the material, usually using a xerographic process or a computer printer. In some cases, books are printed on demand with no inventory kept. This places the bulk of the financial risk for the venture on the creators, with many self-publishers ultimately subsidizing it rather than making money from it.

CHAPTER 1: WHY SELF-PUBLISH

For very low cost (or no cost – I've done it that way!) you can:
- Print an attractive memoir for family and friends
- Publish and sell your own creative writing
- Bring an idea or a cause to the attention of the public (free e-books are ideal for this)

Sell copies of your own book at speaking events publish and sell a book about any topic that interests you

How is publishing-on-demand (POD) different from vanity publishing?
In vanity publishing, you pay to have copies printed and bound. You store, sell, and ship them yourself. The process is expensive, especially if the company formats your manuscript for you.

In POD, copies are printed only when someone wants to buy them. You don't store or ship them. Your book is available from online booksellers, which will give you a free marketing page and opportunities to post a bio, reviews, and a video. Most important, the whole process is free unless you want to pay for professional editing, custom formatting, original cover artwork, or other special services.

And because publish-on-demand services are inexpensive, you can buy copies of your books very cheaply (a boon if you're doing book signings or sending out review copies). If you use CreateSpace, there are even more benefits: a free ISBN, a free marketing page on Amazon.com, a free "Look Inside" marketing feature, and other marketing tools.

CHAPTER 2: BEFORE YOU BEGIN WRITING

- There are a few things that you must know how to do in order even to begin writing your masterpiece. Here are a few tips and tricks to keep in mind while you are creating your book:
- Learn how to use styles in Word software (Normal, Heading 1, Heading 2, indent, and so on)
- Learn as much as you can about Microsoft Word
- Use the settings in your style menu for indentations and other special effects. DO NOT use the tab key or space bar for indentations.

- Familiarize yourself with writing conventions like quotation marks and capital letters
- Have a professional photographer take some digital head shots of you

- Go to an online provider to start a blog free. Or you can have a designer create a WordPress blog for you: www.Wordpress.com. Warning: free blogs don't provide customer service, and you and your followers may have difficulty with access.

- Educate yourself about permissions and copyright

- Consider participating in one or more free social networking sites, such as Facebook (www.Facebook.com) or, if you're a professional, LinkedIn (www.LinkedIn.com).

- Start thinking about friends and colleagues who might write endorsements or a foreword for you

Writing/Formatting Tips:
No matter what publishing option you use, you're going to have to create a publishable manuscript on your own. Do it right the first time to avoid spending days cleaning up your manuscript later (or paying a pile of money for someone to do the job for you).

- Use your computer's spellchecker and grammar checker. They're not infallible, but they're a tremendous help.

- Use only one space (not two) after a period. (You're not in high school any more!).

- Fact-check relentlessly

- Choose the styles you want (Normal, Heading 1, Heading 2, etc.), and monitor them carefully while you're writing.

- Write with the "Look Inside!" feature at Amazon.com in mind. It allows potential buyers to read your table of contents and first chapter online, free. Make sure your table of contents effectively presents your content and unique approach to your topic, and make sure your first

- Use styles to control paragraph indents; don't use a few spaces or a tab to indent the first line of your paragraphs. This can be set in the style definition in Microsoft Word under "first line indent."

- Use styles to control space between paragraphs instead of just hitting Return. You can stipulate this spacing in the paragraph formatting dialog in Word under "Spacing after."

- If you're planning to publish an e-book or Kindle, create a bookmark for your Table of Contents so readers will be able to navigate to it from anywhere in your book. Name this bookmark TOC.

- Don't "Paste" in photos or graphics; use "Insert" instead. This will ensure your photos and graphics get into your eBook with the best resolution. In Word, use the "Insert" menu.

- Use heading styles, not local formatting, for emphasis. Word comes with heading styles, named Heading 1, Heading 2, and so on. Modify them to your liking, then make sure every similar heading is assigned the same style so your book is consistent throughout.

If you're planning to convert your file to an ebook, remember that you'll need to remove any running heads or page numbers you've inserted for the print edition.

Always work on a backup copy of your print book file. You want to end up with two copies of your book: one for CreateSpace to print, the other to be converted to Kindle eBook format using Kindle Direct Publishing.

Find illustrations at www.Google.com by typing in your search term and clicking the Images link. Then click Tools and Usage Rights. Click Labeled for Non-Commercial Uses for copyright-free images. Warning: Not everything that you find there will actually be fair use. Click through for the sources. Wikipedia and Wiki Commons are also wonderful sources for fair-use images.

Consider a paid subscription to Stock.Adobe.com (there's no "www"). You'll get up to 10 images a month, and unused images carry over to the next month.

Building Your Book on Kindle (free) will help you format your manuscript as an e-book.

For 99¢ you can download Alan Shepard's Kindle book From Word to Kindle: Self Publishing, Your Kindle Book with Microsoft Word, or Tips for Formatting Your Text in MS Word So Your Ebook, Doesn't Look Horrible (Like Everyone Else's). If you don't own a Kindle, you can read it on your computer.

I use a paid hosting service for my marketing newsletter: www.ConstantContact.com.

CHAPTER 3: TO MARKET, TO MARKET

Getting the word out about your book is the biggest challenge in any kind of publishing. Even if you're publishing with a big commercial company, you'll have to do most of the marketing yourself. Here are three free marketing strategies:

Write and post articles about your topic at ezinearticles.com (Note: There's no "www"). You can put up to two links at the bottom of each article to send readers to your blog and book page. Your articles will be picked up and republished by online magazines and newsletters.

Publish a short free ebook at www.Smashwords.com. Display your website on the title page. At the end of your book, include a preview (such as the the first chapter) from the book you're trying to sell.

Use the tips in the Smashwords Book Marketing Guide mentioned earlier.

Learn how to set up a blog at www.makeawebsitehub.com. Click the Start a Blog link.

Miscellaneous things self-publishers should know:

Install Word on your computer. Using another word-processing program might cause huge headaches later when you have to convert your files to Word.

Sometimes formatting commands are hidden in the hard return at the end of a paragraph. If formatting problems are driving you crazy, try deleting the hard return at the end of the paragraph, and then re-insert it.

Printed books should have an ISBN (a bookseller's number – but e-books don't need them). ISBNs are free at CreateSpace, Lulu, and Smashwords. Those companies will be listed as the publisher, but you can also put a company name that you make up yourself on the title page. (For example, I use "Maple Leaf Press" for my books.)

If you're using CreateSpace, stick with their free ISBN. I made the mistake of purchasing my own ISBN for a book. It was a waste of money, and schools and libraries had difficulty ordering my book. You'll save yourself some headaches by using the free ISBN.
On Microsoft Word, you'll find a ready-made copyright symbol © in the Insert pull-down menu.

Headers and footers can be a huge headache. To get your page numbers and chapter headings right, insert Section Breaks and click (or unclick) "Same as Previous" in the header/footer menu. Sometimes "Same as Previous" appears (confusingly) in two places in Word. Be sure to find both of them, or your Section Breaks won't work properly. You may have to unclick "Same as Previous" several times. (I wasted hours before I discovered this useful information!)

If you're converting the file for a book manuscript into an ebook, begin by making a new copy of your manuscript file and saving it in .txt or Notepad. (Yes, you'll lose all that lovely formatting!) Then redo your headings by using your style menu, with one important warning: Use the same typeface (such as Times New Roman, Arial, Garamond) for everything.

The style settings in your word processor are your best friends. Set them up carefully to get the look you want for your manuscript. Don't use the tab key ever. Use the space bar only to put a space after a period (one, not two). Never, NEVER underline.

If you want to copy something another person has written, or a picture produced by someone else, you'll need a written permission unless the work is considered "fair use." Often.

CHAPTER 4: KINDLE PUBLISHING

While self-publishing through your own site has its benefits, the massive audience of Amazon's Kindle store makes it appealing for authors looking to share their work with new readers. Publishing for Kindle comes with its own challenges, especially in the design and formatting departments.

Because there are so many people who have important things to write about, things that could help and inspire other people.

YOU are one of those people, even if you've never considered writing a book before. You have a wealth of experience, interests, and ideas accumulated through a lifetime that other people could benefit from. Think about it for a minute. Think about what you know through your career, relationships, hobbies, and life challenges.

You probably take these things for granted, assuming no one would find them useful or interesting. But you're wrong. There are people all over the world searching for the knowledge you could share with them.

So back to that 98% rejection statistic. You might wonder why you'd want to go to the effort of writing a book if the odds of getting it published are so low. Good news future author: you can publish your own book without facing the prospect of a rejection letter.

Self-publishing has changed the entire playing field, and now anyone who has a book inside of them can get it out, publish it, and sell it.

However, just because you can self-publish doesn't mean you should throw out a crappy book and expect it to sell. But you wouldn't want to do that anyway. Self-publishing gives you the opportunity to present your book to the world, but you have to seize the opportunity by producing a quality book that people will want to buy.

Can you do that?

Whatever self-doubts you have at the moment about writing and publishing a book, set them aside as you read through this post, and challenge yourself to make writing and publishing a book one of your goals for the year.

These are your words, this is your story; a tale of pathos and woe, heartbreak and longing, action, violence, sex, death and transformation. Its overarching message will no doubt resonate deeply with the reader.

In order to have readers, your work must be published. Luckily, this is now easy to do for practically anyone. Where once writers had to rely upon agents and publishers to consider their work; anyone can publish their novel, essay, or non-fiction masterpiece on Amazon's Kindle platform.

Why Choose Kindle?

The Kindle is a series of eReaders and tablets offered by Amazon. In parallel, the company has also constructed an entire eBook publishing platform that allows authors—any author—to reach potentially more than a billion readers around the world.

Along with the Kindle device, a Kindle app is available for nearly every major web browser, smartphone platform and for both Windows and Mac-based computers. Publish your work once via Amazon's "Kindle Direct Publishing" platform and it instantly becomes available through the Kindle app on nearly any personal computing device.

Another reason to publish with Amazon's Kindle platform is the fact that Amazon dominates the "eBook" market.

Finally, even for those with minimal computing skills, publishing on Amazon's Kindle platform is relatively pain-free.

1. Decide On KDP Select Vs. KDP

Your first hurdle is deciding between Kindle Direct Publishing and KDP Select. Both connect your work with the millions of Kindle owners and readers who use Kindle apps on their smartphones and tablets. Both offer 70 percent royalties for books priced $2.99 to $9.99.

The big difference is that KDP Select requires 100 percent exclusivity — your digital book cannot be sold anywhere else.

While there's a lot of debate about the merits of KDP Select, it was the clear choice for this book for several reasons:

Experiment: Alexis wanted to see whether KDP was a worthwhile complement to her own online store, with the goal of gaining exposure to a new audience of Kindle owners and using the Amazon algorithms to boost sales. Rather than dilute the test by publishing on a variety of platforms, we opted to go with KDP alone, so the exclusivity clause didn't bother us.

Effort: Instead of spreading our efforts across several platforms, we opted to focus our energy on only one to maximize the returns.

Promotion options: KDP Select allows you to either offer the book free for five days or discount it for up to seven days through a Countdown Deal, which appealed to us — especially since during a CD, you still earn 70 percent royalties. You can run promotions manually if you're in KDP, but once you price your book below $2.99, you'll only get 35 percent.

Lending Library: All KDP Select books are included in the Kindle Owners' Lending Library, which is free for Amazon Prime members. Every time your book is borrowed, you earn a share of a monthly fund ($1.2M in April 2014). While the fund wasn't a huge draw, we were curious to see how many times the book would be borrowed. No earth-shattering results here: we only had five borrows in February and March 2014.

Choosing whether to use KDP Select or publish on more than one platform is an individual decision; you'll have to figure out what makes sense for your work. One author who has made KDP Select work well for him is Steve Scott, who has had 39 books in the program. One benefit he mentions is that with so many books, he could choose to constantly run Countdown Deals, which leads to greater exposure for the rest of his catalogue.

2. Design And Refine Your Cover

Your cover is a crucial element of your e-book; it's all that Amazon will show potential buyers who scan Top 100 lists and "Customers Who Bought This Item Also Bought." While we have a designer on the Socialexis team, we've also had good experiences using crowdsourcing sites like 99designs or Crowdspring.

Your cover must look good even when it's tiny: your book's page shows a 160px by 250px version, while the "Customers Who Bought This Item Also Bought" covers measure only 60px by 90px. Bright colors, bold text and a defined image help create an appealing cover. You'll need a 1563px by 2500px image; Amazon recommends a 1.6 height: width ratio.

One way to make sure your cover resonates with potential readers is to have your designer create two or three options, then ask your audience for feedback. This not only lets you see whether there's a clear preference, it also clues you into small details you might not have considered. Alexis' readers chose the final design and shared valuable feedback that helped us make the cover more attractive.

3. Convert Your Manuscript To Mobi

While you can technically upload formats including .doc, RTF, PDF, txt, ePub and HTML, most experts recommend uploading your book as a mobi, a format specific to Kindle. DIY'ing the conversion can be time-consuming — you want to make sure everything's perfect! — but it's worth it to learn the process so you'll save time on future books.

First, download Amazon's free programs KindleGen and Kindle Previewer. KindleGen converts HTML files to mobi, while Kindle Previewer shows you how your book will appear on different versions of the Kindle.

Next, open Scrivener and get ready for it to blow your mind. Once you tell Scrivener where to find KindleGen, its Compile function handles the conversion for you — all you have to do is specify formatting choices.

While there will be lots of trial and error — I went through at least 25 test conversions — it's worth it to play with different settings and see what looks best for your book. Each conversion took fewer than 10 seconds; most of your time will be spent reviewing in the Kindle Previewer and tweaking Scrivener's Compile settings.

Few tips: don't include a cover in your Compile, since you'll upload it to Amazon separately. Scrivener can automatically create a Table of Contents that links to each chapter during the Compile; just check the box under HTML Settings. Choose whether you want it centered, which is the default, or left-aligned; if the latter, go to Layout and uncheck the box next to "center the TOC."

If your chapters have complicated names and structure like Alexis' book, make a TOC manually using Scrivener links, which you'll find under Edit –> Scrivener Link –> New Link; then check the "Convert Scrivener Links to HTML links" box under HTML Settings to turn these into regular hyperlinks when you hit Compile.

For a detailed walk through the process, read Patrick Hester's Scrivener Quick Tips Series, especially the posts on Building an Ebook. Ed Ditto also explains how quick and easy the process can be in his guest post on The Book Designer, and the Google+ Scrivener Users Community is extraordinarily helpful. If you don't have Scrivener, its creators offer a 30-day free trial (that's 30 days of use, not 30 days from download) and it's available for both Windows and Mac users.

4. Publish And Set Price On Amazon

Before you get to the technical aspects of uploading and publishing your book, consider the strategic side of the process. Upload your book at least 48 hours before you plan to launch

Jeff Goins recommends publishing your book on Amazon a few weeks before your ideal launch date, then sending free copies to friends, family, colleagues and bloggers in your field and asking them to leave a review on the book's Amazon page. That way, when you tell the world about your book, prospective buyers will see lots of positive reviews — a big factor for those who may not be familiar with your work.

Also recommends sending out 150 to 200 free review copies, we only sent about 20, which resulted in 11 reviews by launch day. We probably could've spent more time on this, but those reviews seemed to do the trick.

Uploading your book is actually quite simple. Choose your two categories carefully: these sections of the Kindle bookstore help potential buyers find your book while browsing and on Top 100 lists. We chose Careers –> Job Hunting and Careers –> Guides and have seen a marked difference: the book has consistently ranked higher in Job Hunting because Guides includes more heavy-hitters in the career advice world (think The 4-Hour Workweek and The $100 Startup). We did hit #1 in both categories, though.

Add up to seven keywords that will lead readers to your book. Be thoughtful about this: What terms will potential buyers search for in the Kindle store? What questions does your book answer? Upload your cover and choose whether you want Digital Rights Management protection for your book.

Congratulations, you're ready to actually upload your book! Click "Browse" and select your mobi file. Once it has loaded, check it one more time with the Online Previewer, then click "Save & Continue" to move on to the Pricing section. Your royalty options depend on the price you choose.

5. Reward Your Loyal Audience (Very Important)

Your first buyers on Kindle are likely part of your existing audience: blog readers, social media followers and friends. Reward these people who know, enjoy and support your work by giving them a great deal.

You Deserve to Love Your Job launched at $0.99 before jumping to its $4.99 regular price, so the 123 people who bought in the first 24 hours got a great deal.

Incentivizing early purchasers also has another effect: when lots of people purchase at once, Amazon's algorithm picks up on your book and promotes it, exposing it to more potential buyers and helping your book climb the ranks.

6. Promote Your Book

While Amazon will help your book reach new readers, its algorithm requires the book to first hit a certain (mysterious) number of sales. To earn support from Amazon, you need to spread the word about your book yourself. However, your efforts can't end after launch: plan to continue marketing your book for as long as you want to make sales.

What's the best way to do that? Write and submit guest posts that support your book. Share important quotes on social media; we created quote images for several of the book's sound bites. Continue to link to your book in your blog posts, social media updates and email signature. Plan promotions: remember that for each 90-day KDP Select cycle, you get either five Free Days or one seven-day Countdown Deal. Get creative to market your book to new buyers.

7. Track Your Metrics

You want to see results from all this hard work, right?

Use a simple spreadsheet to track your book's performance (we use Google docs). Here's what we measure:

Sales: Your KDP Report only shows month-to-date sales; if you want daily sales, track them yourself by checking this report every 24 hours. Since this is an experiment, we track sales in all countries, and we've been surprised at the numbers from outside North America — hello, buyers in the UK, Denmark, Spain and Australia!

Borrows: Because the book is in the Kindle Owners Lending Library, it earns a portion of a monthly pool based on its number of borrows. Borrows also contribute to the book's rankings; Amazon's algorithm treats them like sales. Borrows appear in the same month-to-date sales report and we track them monthly.

Reviews: Check your book's sales page to see how many reviews it has earned and what readers think. We track the number of reviews of each star rating and note any recurring feedback on a weekly basis.

Rank: While some Kindle experts like Steve Scott discourage tracking rank (in his Kindle book Is $.99 the New Free?), we consider it part of the experiment. Check your book's sales page under "Product Details" to see its rank overall in the Kindle store and in each of its categories. Rankings are updated hourly; be careful not to get sucked into hitting Refresh every few minutes!

With these advantages in mind, here is the step-by-step guide to self-publishing your own works with Amazon's tools.

1. Sign Up To Publish
At the bottom of Amazon's home page is a link to "independently publish with us." Click the link. You are ready to publish to Kindle.

2. Create Kindle Publishing Account
Click "Get Started" to begin.

You will need to use your existing Amazon account or create one. Note: You may be required to provide additional information, including your banking information, as Amazon will wire your royalties to your account on a quarterly basis.

3. Add Title
With an account created, Amazon takes you to your "Kindle Dashboard." This is where you will add your works and access reports on book sales. If your work is ready to be published, click on "Add New Title."

4. Enter Your Book Details
Here, you provide Amazon with details on your book, including title, authorship, book type, pricing and more. Note: You do not need to have an ISBN code when using Amazon.

5. Book Category
Amazon encourages you to add up to two "categories" for your book. This1 can include everything from "Body, Mind & Spirit" to "Dystopian Fiction."
Recommendation: Chances are your book crosses more than two categories. Search Amazon for the book(s) that you think is most like yours. In the details page, Amazon includes the categories selected for that book.

You can also add up to seven keywords.

Recommendation: Think of the words readers might use to find your work in a search string. Choose those words. If it is a book about Steve Jobs, for example, you might include: Steve Jobs, Apple, iPhone, Macintosh, Silicon Valley, Ashton Kutcher, iPad.

6. Give Your Book a Cover

Even an eBook should have a cover, although it is not required.

Amazon provides guidelines for uploading cover images and also includes a rather limited tool to create your own cover.

Recommendation: I strongly encourage you to hire someone to create a visually appealing cover for your work if you don't have the skills for this. Services such as eLance can connect you with graphic designers at affordable prices.

A poor cover image is likely to turn away potential buyers.

7. Time To Upload Your Book

Now comes the fun-scary part: uploading your book!

Luckily, Amazon makes this rather easy. First, it asks you to choose if you will enable digital rights management (DRM) or not. If you enable DRM, this makes it harder for others to share your work and potentially harder for it to be copied and sold without payment.

Odds are very high that you will never lose sales (or money) because your eBook did not have DRM enabled. My recommendation is to go DRM-free. Click "do not enable digital rights management."

Now upload the book from your computer.

Amazon accepts the following formats:

- Word (DOC and DOCX)
- HTML
- ePub

- Text
- PDF

8. Formatting and Previewing

If your work has minimal formatting requirements—it looks like a normal work of fiction or non-fiction, for example—Amazon's upload service is extremely good at retaining your formatting. Nonetheless, you should still preview your work even after successfully uploading it.

If your work contains numerous images, for example, and/or charts or other special formatting requirements, you may need to use a special program for that and then save the document in PDF format. Amazon's upload service should retain the proper formatting.

Recommendation: It's still best to always remember that an eBook is presented on a screen. Screens come in many sizes – from iPad Mini's to iPhones to a new BlackBerry and many others. Works that include multiple graphics, say, may simply never look as good on a electronic screen as they do in print.

After uploading your work, use the "Online Previewer" link to see how your book will look on different devices. Then, from the drop down list, Amazon lets you see what your book will look like on select Kindle devices, iPhone and iPad. If you wish to see how it will look on other devices, or in a browser, you will need to download the "previewer" tool.

9. Set Your Price

Amazon lets you set nearly any price you wish for your book. However, there are two different royalty options: 35% or 70%. Obviously, you want the 70% royalty.

In nearly all cases, choosing the 70% royalty is the wise decision. Know this, however:

If you price your book below $2.99, Amazon will only offer the 35% royalty option.

In some smaller markets, Amazon only offers the 35% royalty. (The 70% option is available in the U.S., Canada, UK and most larger markets.)

When you choose the 70% royalty option, Amazon also deducts a small "delivery fee" for each book sold. This is their additional fee for wirelessly distributing your work, and is based on the file size of your work. In the U.S., this fee is presently set at 15 cents per megabyte. (A Word document of approximately 100,000 words and with minimal graphics is typically no more than 1 MB.)

There is no delivery charge with the 35% royalty option.

Thus, if you charge $2.99 for your work and choose the 70% royalty option, your royalty for each book sold is likely to be:

$2.99 x .70 = $2.09 before delivery fee

$2.09 – .15 (delivery fee) = $1.94.

You earn $1.94 for each book sold. (Authors are solely responsible for paying taxes.) You can designate your book for sale in only certain countries, or worldwide.

10. Finished!
Congratulations! You are no longer just an author, but an author whose book(s) is available across the world. Of course, it typically takes Amazon about 24-48 hours before your book is actually available for sale.

Once available, I also recommend you create an Amazon author page – a free service that links your bio with your book listing.

Some final notes. Throughout this process, Amazon somewhat aggressively promotes their "KDP Select" program. With KDP Select, if you agree to publish your work on Kindle—exclusively—for 90 days (this can vary) and allow Amazon customers to borrow it for free, Amazon will pay you a small fee each time the book is borrowed. Typically, this fee is close to the royalty you would have received had the book actually been purchased.

Amazon obviously wants everyone to have their work available exclusively through Amazon.

Given Amazon's market share, you may wish to join KDP Select. Of course, this does preclude those who prefer to use Apple's iBooks service, or other platform, from buying your work for three months.

Kindle Direct Publishing – Top 4 Reasons To Start Today!

If you are looking to make money online, there's probably no better way to start than with Kindle publishing. It's relatively easy and cheap to get started compared to other ways to make money online. Before you jump on any other method to earn money online, consider Kindle publishing first.

1.Low barrier to entry

Kindle Publishing is especially attractive for starters because of the low barrier to entry. If you've been looking for ways to make side income online but are limited on budget, Kindle publishing is for you. Practically anyone can publish so long as you have some creativity and common sense.

For instance, with a measly $200, you can hit the ground going and you can expect returns in the first month. Once your book is up, you start earning right away. Chances are you will recoup your investment within a couple of months.

That said, the ideal starter budget for Kindle publishing is about $1500. There are a couple of things you need to get right when you're starting to guarantee some sales. Marketing is of utmost importance, and for this, you're going to need some training. In fact, a big chunk of your startup cash is going to be invested in quality education. This is something that cannot be overlooked, but don't worry as it's worth it in the end.

In addition, you need to publish at least two books right off the bat. Since it is highly unlikely (but possible) that your first book will be a bestseller, it is a good idea to publish more than one.

There's a bigger chance that one of your books will be a success and if so, you will get buoyed by that success and you can replicate the winning formula to create other books.

2. Easily Scalable

Once your book starts raking in the cash, you can reinvest the money into writing new books. With more cash to spend, you can outsource many of the tasks involved so that you focus on creating new ideas and marketing your books. You can outsource the writing, cover design, and pretty much anything else you do to get the book published.

The unique thing about Kindle publishing is that it offers more than one way to earn from a single book. For instance, you can publish the same book on Createspace and also publish an audio version on ACX. That's one asset with three streams of income. You can do this for all your books and the money starts to add up quickly.

One thing to note is that you need to scale if you want to make a six-figure income from Kindle publishing. For instance, good, experienced publishers make between $150 to $300 per book per month. To get to your dream six-figure, you need to be able to scale quickly.

Bottom line is that it can be done. Remember there's no limit to how many books you can publish. All you need to do is repeat and refine what works.

3. No Skills Needed

This is one of the top-most reasons to start with Kindle publishing. You don't need any specific skill to get started. You do need a good topic, however, and good marketing know-how, which you can get from a high-quality marketing course.

You also need to learn the basics of how to start publishing on Kindle. There's a lot of great info online to help you get started. But seriously consider paid courses for higher quality information. Whatever you choose, here is where you should put your learning emphasis towards:

-How to choose a good topic.
-How to generate book ideas.
-How to plan a portfolio strategy for Kindle publishing and why it is key to your publishing success.
-The top marketing strategies for Kindle publishing.
-How to find the best ghostwriters to outsource your book writing tasks.

The best part is that once you have a couple of books published, you become comfortable with the process. You can then refine your methods and increase your success.

Once again, the best part of this process is that you do not need to actually be skilled in anything! Not good at writing? Outsource! Not good at graphic design? Outsource! Not good at copywriting? Outsource!

4. Good Passive Income

There are many ways to earn passive income online. However, most require a lot of time invested especially when you are starting from scratch. Not so with Kindle publishing. The income from Kindle publishing is pretty much passive once the book is uploaded. It is true income on autopilot.

As already said, to reach true autopilot status that guarantees more than $1000 in monthly sales, you need to scale. Producing many quality books quickly is the key to scaling up. A premium ghost writer costs up to $1000 per book but you don't need to spend that much for the purpose of making money. Spend some time searching and you will land a descent writer at $1 per 100 words, or go with a ghost writing service.

The same technique works for cover design and the description parts. Outsource and get the work done fast.

Scan through the Kindle store daily. Browse best sellers in the different categories. You want to develop an eye for design for your own cover designs. The big majority of users on Amazon are impulse buyers so learn how to use colors and lettering that grabs attention. The best part of having a Kindle business is that once it is built up, it doesn't require a lot of work to upkeep. You can choose to continue releasing books or not, or you can kick back and watch the royalties roll in on the books you already have.

Wrapping Up
Publishing on Kindle has immense potential. With Amazon's giant paid search engine, you have instant access to thousands of potential buyers.

There's simply no better time to earn from self-publishing than now. E-book sales are in billions yearly and have been rising steadily. Get started now and claim your share of the pie. The best way to achieve success with Kindle publishing is to replicate what successful publishers have done.

CHAPTER 5: SELF PUBLISH YOUR BOOK WITH AMAZON'S CREATESPACE

CreateSpace is the publishing engine of global online retailer and publisher Amazon, the company everyone either wants to love or hate. Createspace began life in 2002 as CustomFlix Labs (DVD), originally intended to make widespread distribution easier for independent filmmakers by providing on-demand DVD production. In 2000, a small group of writers pooled resources to form Booksurge with the intention of creating opportunities for authors to self-publish their books and retain content rights and sales profits. Both companies ⬜uickly flourished and in 2005, Amazon acquired them, with CustomFlix Labs changing its name to CreateSpace in 2007.

By late 2009, Amazon took the logical step and merged CreateSpace and Booksurge under the CreateSpace brand name to form a single company offering on-demand manufacturing of books, DVD's and music formats for independent artists and businesses. CreateSpace also support on-demand products for Amazon retail and their publishing imprints AmazonEncore (for deserving author slipping under the mainstream radar) and AmazonCrossing (for foreign language books deserving an English translation).

CreateSpace offer access to a thriving online community of CreateSpace authors well worth browsing if any author is seriously considering using this service. CreateSpace offers an abundance of other services from design and layout to editing, but again, CreateSpace's strength lies in being a provider of DIY self-publishing services for authors who can provide print ready files and I would like to think that they will not go the way of Lulu and start to place more of an emphasis on some of the expensive packages listed above.

CreateSpace is now at the forefront of DIY self-publishing and the introduction of the Pro-Plan at $39 makes it a difficult choice to ignore. Short of working with Ingram's Lightning Source (a more complex undertaking for the DIY self-publisher), CS beats

Lulu hands down on front end pricing, and lacks some of the frustrations authors experience with Smashwords.

The truth is, print-on-demand publishing is the fastest, most profitable and easiest way to get your written thoughts out there. Today, self-published books are even distributed to traditional outlets like Barnes & Noble and academic libraries. Most people searching Amazon or shopping the book shelves don't even think to question whether the book was self-published or printed by a publishing company. They wouldn't ever know unless they checked the product details.

Of course, self-publishing means you don't get the marketing resources that come with a traditional publishing deal, but in our world of social media, that can be easily fixed. So if self publishing is so easy, why don't we see more authors using it? Most people are simply not aware of the low barrier to entry.

After evaluating the various options, I chose CreateSpace. It met my needs the best, but your mileage may vary, so research your options careful and pick the service that matches best with your goals and the type of book you plan to publish.

Here Is A Step-By-Step Guide To Publishing Your Own Book Using Createspace:

1: Create
When writing your book, make sure it has all the necessary parts: introduction, acknowledgments, dedication, resources, table of contents and copyright page. If you choose to prepare the files yourself, as opposed to using CreateSpace professional services, you need to make sure to set up the appropriate margins, headers, page numbers and other formatting elements. To make things easier, the site offers ready-to-print templates that you can download for free and use to write your book. When you're ready, you'll simply export a PDF and have a print-ready file.

2: Setup

Once you've completed the writing process, you can easily set up a new book in your CreateSpace account. The setup process guides you through simple steps of inputting the book title, description, and credits, choosing the book size and paper color, and finally, uploading the files (one for the interior, one for the cover).

While the interior file is relatively easy to create yourself using a template, the cover of your book may be a little more challenging. Again, the site offers a variety of solutions for beginners (such as building a simple cover using their online Cover Creator tool) and advanced authors alike.

Finally, you'll choose your book's ISBN number. I decided to go with a free CreateSpace assigned ISBN. Unless you are planning on re-publishing or distributing your book with a traditional publisher in the future, or would like to choose your own publisher company name, there isn't really any value to paying $99 for your own ISBN.

3: Review

Now it's time to submit your book for a review. At this point, the CreateSpace team looks at every file and checks for potential issues before approving for print. If they see something set up incorrectly, they will email you the notes so you have a chance to re-submit your file. For example, I included color text and special characters that wouldn't print correctly, and the review team caught both and sent me an email. The review process usually takes up to 24 hours, after which you can order a physical proof copy to check over before putting your book for sale.

The community section of the site warns all first-time authors that they might need to view multiple proofs of their book until they're satisfied. It's helpful to have at least two to three other people reading the printed copy of your book — each might discover separate issues that the others hadn't noticed.

4: Distribute

Once you are ready to hit "approve" on your proof, you can set up the distribution information for your title and select your sales channels. This is where you'll set up your book's price and calculate royalties based on the book's size, number of pages and type of paper. From the research I've done, CreateSpace provides the highest profits on a standard trade type book, however I suggest playing with their royalty calculator before you decide on the format and size of your book. For example, after increasing the font size of my book I discovered that it added 20 pages, which resulted in almost $0.50 less royalties per book.

CreateSpace does not offer a hardcover option at this point, so if that's a deal breaker, you'll have to choose another platform (like Lulu) to publish your book. For most independent authors, because hardcover books cost more to print, you may not be able to profit from them, which is something to consider. It's a decision that not only affects your retail price and royalties, but also the personal cost to buy your own book for press promotions.

After finalizing the price, you can choose one or more distribution channels. There's the CreateSpace eStore, where you can market your book directly with a customizable product page, Amazon.com or Expanded Distribution Channel. The last option requires a pro plan upgrade.The pro plan has a one-time fee of $39 with a $5 renewal fee each year thereafter. It makes your book available to thousands of retail and online outlets, including Barnes & Noble, libraries and more. Although there is no guarantee these stores will actually pick up your book, at least it will be included in a distribution list. While the eStore listing is created immediately, Amazon listings take about five to seven business days. Expanded distribution may take a few weeks.

Once Amazon creates the initial listing, you can update it with additional information or edits via Amazon Author Central (this requires opening an author account). Here you can actually create a nice author page with your full bio and headshot, which may help your sales. In my experience, Amazon was responsive and kind when dealing with my requests. From applying edits to my title within hours to personally answering my first-time author questions via provided phone support, I was supplied with consistent help throughout the entire process.

If you're planning a digital release, it might actually make sense to delay the release and encourage people to get the paperback first. Releasing a digital version of your book could be a great reason for a secondary marketing push, so plan it wisely. You can use the CreateSpace conversion service for Kindle ($69, takes about 2 weeks) or spend a couple of hours reformatting the book yourself, then converting it into a .prc file using one of the many free downloadable tools. From there, just upload it into Amazon's Kindle Direct Publishing site. If your title is already listed on Amazon, the Kindle version will be automatically matched.

Converting to iPad is a similar process. Convert your files to ePUB and upload your book to iTunes. CreateSpace doesn't help much so you'll need to use a competitor like Lulu.

5: Sales & Marketing

Once your title is listed, all that's left to do is to let people know about it! Here again CreateSpace supplies a suite of on-demand marketing solutions from a press release to video trailers. Amazon also offers up-to-date sales reports so you can track how well your book is selling. Of course, traditional social media marketing techniques apply here as well. You should certainly lean on you pre-existing social networks to promote your book.

Considering the ease and effectiveness of the self-publishing process, I'm sure we'll be seeing more and more self-published books in the next few years. At this point self-publishing still remains an uncharted territory for independent content creators, which means it's the perfect time to get on board.

CHAPTER 6: HOW TO PUBLISH A BOOK

Publishing a book might seem even more daunting than writing one. But with the right guidance, all is possible! To publish your book, you have to make sure it's in the best possible shape before you take it to agents or publishers. Publishing your book will take a lot of research, perseverance, and patience, but it will be worth it to see your work in print. If you want to know how to publish your book, just follow these easy steps.

1. Know whether you should prepare a manuscript or a proposal. Fiction writers should prepare a full-length manuscript, while non-fiction writers will have to write a solid book proposal instead. Knowing what you need to have written will save you time and will make you look more professional when you send your work out into the world.

Many fiction writers try to publish their books before they have completed a manuscript — to no avail. If you are a seasoned writer working with a literary agent, then just a few chapters or even a proposal can get you a contract, but for most people starting out in the fiction business, the book should be 100% done before moving forward to the publication stage.

If you're writing non-fiction, then you need to have a completed book proposal first. If you are writing a fitness book or a cookbook, then you should focus on the proposal. If you're working on more literary non-fiction, then you should work on more sample chapters or even a completed manuscript, in some cases.

If you have determined that you only need a proposal for the type of nonfiction you are writing, then skip to step 6 and decide whether you want to hire a literary agent or go directly to the publishing house.
If you are writing an academic textbook, then skip to the last section and learn how to publish your book by contacting a publisher directly.

2. Revise your book. Revising your book can be even trickier than finishing it. Once you've written a solid draft of your book, whether it's a historical novel or a thriller, you'll

need to revise it so it's in the best shape possible before you take it to an agent or publishing house. Here are some things to do as you revise your book:

Make sure your book is as engaging as possible. Though not every book is a spy novel or a page turner, make sure your readers are hooked from the beginning, and that they always have a reason to keep turning those pages.

Get rid of any wordiness or excess. Many agents say that they rarely accept a debut novelist's book if it's over 100,000 words.

Make sure you get your point across. Whether you're writing a romance novel or science fiction, you should have reached your objective and communicated your message by the end of the book.

Make sure your thoughts are as clear as possible. Your ideas may be crystal clear to you, but would they confuse your average reader? Of course, your book may be targeted toward a certain audience, but members of that audience (such as college students or nurses) should be able to clearly follow your thoughts.

3. Get feedback on your book. Once you think you're really done, it's important to get some feedback on your book to know if it's ready for publication. You may feel that it's absolutely perfect, but there is almost always room for improvement. It's better to get feedback from a fellow writer or trusted professional than to get rejected by an agent or publisher. If you ask for feedback too early in the drafting process, you may feel stifled, so make sure your book feels really ready before you ask for help. Here are some ways to get feedback on your book:

Ask a fellow writer. A friend who knows how to write will have some insight into what works and what does not work in a book.

Ask a voracious reader. Someone who reads a lot will be able to tell you if your book was a page turner, or if they were asleep after the first chapter.

Ask someone who knows your subject. If you're writing non-fiction about something in a field such as business, science, or cooking, ask someone who is an expert in this field to see if you really know your stuff.

Submit your stuff to a writing workshop. Whether you have an informal writer's workshop with friends in your area or you're attending a writing conference, submitting a chapter of your work to a workshop can give you insight into a variety of perspectives at once.

If you're in an M.A. or M.F.A. program in creative writing, you will have lots of resources for feedback, whether it's your classmates or faculty.
Find a reputable editor and ask for a manuscript evaluation. This can be very expensive, but asking the right person can help you see if your book is ready.

Remember to take your feedback with a grain of salt. Not everyone will fall in love with your book, and that's okay. It's important to get constructive feedback from people you trust, but recognize that you won't benefit from every opinion. Getting good feedback means knowing who to ask.

4. Revise your book further if it's necessary. Revise your book based on the feedback you received. You won't regret it. Take some time to absorb the feedback you received, and then get to work.

Though your revision should take you in the right direction, you should ask for more feedback to make sure you made the draft stronger.

When you've revised your manuscript again, put it away for a few weeks or even a month. Then take it out and read it with fresh eyes to see if it's in the best possible shape.

Last, copy edit your book. Once all of the larger points are taken care of, make sure your manuscript is free of grammatical and punctuation errors. These errors will make your work look unprofessional and will keep your readers from appreciating your hard work.

5. Prepare your manuscript. Once you feel that your manuscript is completely ready, you'll have to format it so it meets the requirements of the agents or publishers you are seeking. There are a few rules of thumb you can follow, but you should also check the websites of the publishers or the agents' guidelines to ensure that your manuscript meets their standards. Here are a few things you can do:
Always double-space your manuscript.

Have one-inch margins on the left and right-hand sides of the manuscript.

No fancy fonts. Times New Roman is the best font to use. Courier, or the font that looks like a typewriter, used to be more prominent, but TNR will do just fine.

Number your pages. Number the pages of your manuscript on the top right-hand side, along with your last name and title before the page number.
Ex: "Smith/WHITE SKY/1"

Have a cover page. The cover page should include the following:

Your name, email address, phone number, and address should appear on the left hand side of the page.

The title of your novel should be capitalized and centered on the page, along with your last name. Example: "WHITE SKY" on one line and "a novel by John Smith" written directly below it.

Your word count should be centered on the bottom of the page. You can round to the nearest 5,000 words. You can write, "about 75,000" words.

6. Decide whether you want to enlist the help of a literary agent or to go straight to the publisher. Though signing with a literary agent is incredibly challenging, contacting a publishing house directly to try to publish your book is even tougher.

The benefit of working directly with a publisher is that you don't have to use (or pay) an agent as a middleman. The drawback is that the publishing houses trust the agents to screen the submissions, so if you don't have an agent, they will be less likely to consider you.

You can also try literary agents first and go to the publisher if it doesn't work out. However, if your work is rejected by many literary agents, it's even more likely to be rejected by the publishers.

Publishing Your Book With The Help Of A Literary Agent

1. Research the market. Once you're ready to take your book to agents, you need to research the market to find your niche. Find books in your field or genre to see where you fit in, and see how well these books are selling and who are big names in your field. If your book doesn't neatly fit in one genre, research multiple types of books that your book may be like.

Once you've researched the market, you should be able to find a way to neatly describe your book. Is it science fiction, literary, or historical? Is it a science fiction and a historical novel? Is it literary, or more of a young adult novel? Knowing what kind of book you have will help you contact the right agent.

2. Research literary agents. Now that you know what type of agent you're working with, it's time for you to find the perfect agent to represent you. The ideal agent will connect with your material, will be enthusiastic about your work, and will work with you to revise your book and sell it to a publisher. Make sure your agent sells books in your genre, or contacting that agent will be a waste of time. Here is how to find a good agent for you:

Read a reputable guide to Literary Agents. This book will tell you more about thousands of literary agents and will also say which genres they specialize in, how many new clients they take on each year, and how many recent sales they have made.

Check out Publisher's Marketplace. Though you'll have to pay $25 a month for full access to the site, you will gain insight into which agents made recent sales, what type of books they sold, and who is selling the most books.

Check out Query Tracker. This site will help you see which agents respond to queries quickly, and which rarely respond or take months to respond. The statistics on this site are reported by other writers, so the data set isn't complete, but it can give you a good indication of how receptive some agents can be. The site can also tell you which agents specialize in what genres.

Check out the websites of different agents. When you find an agent who sounds like a good fit, check out his or her website to get more information about submission policies and what genres and clients they represent.

Make sure the agent is accepting unsolicited submissions. Unless you have a connection, you'll have to submit to the agent this way.

Watch out for con-artists posing as agents. No reputable agent will ever ask for a reading fee to see your manuscript. The agent will only make money if he can sell your book. Check out Preditors & Editors to make sure the agent has a good rating.

3. Write a Query letter. Once you've found your dream agent — or better yet, a handful of dream agents — it's time to prepare your Query letter. Your Query letter is your chance to introduce yourself to the agent, to get the agent hooked on your book, and to provide a very brief synopsis of the book. It can take a while to hear back from agents, so contact a few at a time (as long as they allow simultaneous submissions) and sit back and wait. The query letter should follow the following format:

Paragraph one: an introduction of your book and your interest in the agent. Here is what should go in the first paragraph:

Start off with one or two sentences that gives the agent a "blurb" of what your book is about. It should be specific, original, and gripping.

Then, tell the agent what genre your book falls under, whether it's multi-cultural, young adult, or historical. It can fall into a number of categories. You should mention the word count in the first paragraph as well.

Tell the agent why you've chosen her. Does she represent a lot of books in your genre, or does she represent a few authors whose work is similar to yours? Do you have a personal connection to the agent? If so, mention it right away.

Paragraph two: a synopsis of your book. Here is what should go in the synopsis:

Describe what happens in your book and what themes are highlighted. Make the description as accurate and gripping as possible.

Show who the main characters are, what the stakes are, and why the book is important. You can do this in one or two paragraphs at most.

Paragraph three: some brief information about yourself. Tell the agent if you've won any awards and how the book personally connects to your life.

Paragraph four: tell the agent that the full manuscript or sample chapters (if you're writing non-fiction) are available upon request and give your contact information. Thank the agent for taking the time to consider your work.
 Follow directions carefully. If the agent also asks for an outline or sample chapters, send those along too.

4. If you get an offer with an agent, sign a contract — if it feels right. If the agent liked your query letter, he or she will ask you to send along some sample chapters or even the whole manuscript. If the agent falls in love with your work after that, you will receive what you've been dreaming about: an offer of representation! But before you sign with the agent, you have to make sure he really is the dream agent you've been seeking.

Talk to the agent over the phone. If you can, meet with the agent in person. If you live near Manhattan, this will be easier, since many literary agents are based in New York City. Get a sense of this person's character and how enthusiastic he is about your book.

Trust your gut. If something is telling you the agent sounds too busy, too eager to get off the phone, or not very excited about your work, don't sign with him. It's better to continue your agent search than to put your book in the hands of the wrong person.

Ask if you can talk to some of the agent's clients. A good agent will be glad to give you the names of a few of his clients, so you can chat with them and get a better sense of whether or not the agent is a good fit.

Double-check your research. Make sure the agent has made sales and has a solid client list before you get on board.
Read over your contract carefully. Once you see that the contract is pretty standard, and that the agent gets around a 15% of your domestic sales and 20% of your foreign

sales, and you feel good about signing with the agent, then sign your contract, put it in the mail, and celebrate a job well done.

5. Revise with the agent. Even if your agent is bowled over by your book, you will almost always have to revise the book once, twice, or even three times before it's ready to go to the market. You'll have to do things like trim down the word count, make your narrator more likable, and address any questions your agent may have.

Remember that the book is still yours and that you don't have to change it completely to suit the needs of the agent. Only make changes that you're comfortable with.

6. Take your book to the market. Once your agent is happy with your manuscript, and you have prepared a package for the book, she will take it to the publishers. This is the most nerve-wracking part because your book's fate will be out of your hands. Your agent will pitch your book to a list of trusted editors at various publishers, and if you're lucky, you'll end up with a deal with an editor at a publishing house!

Sign the contract that includes you, your agent, and the publishing house.

7. Work with an editor. Now that your book has been sold, you'll sign with a publishing house and will continue to work to revise the book with an editor there. You'll work until the writing is exactly where it should be, and then other aspects of publishing will be decided, such as when and how the book will be released, and what the cover will look like.

But you can't just sit tight and wait for the publication date. There is more work to be done!

8. Market your book. Once the fact that your book will be published has sunk in, you'll need to work your butt off to market your book, whether it's through your publicist, your

website, Facebook, informal readings, and word of mouth. Do what you have to do to get the word out there so your sales are high when the book does come out.

Don't ever stop advertising for your book — especially not after it is published. You can bask in your glory for a little while, but remember that promoting your book is just as important as writing it!

Publishing Your Book by Contacting the Publisher Directly

1. Research publishers. Check out the websites of different publishing houses to see if they accept query letters or if they only accept solicitations from agents. Many publishing houses only accept work that has been brought to them through an agent.

Find publishers that not only accept unagented submissions, but which specialize in the type of book you are writing.

2. Write a query letter to the right publishers. The method for writing a query letter for a publishing house is the same as it is for contacting an agent. You'll have to introduce your book as well as yourself and to provide a brief synopsis of the work.

If the publishing house is impressed by your letter, you will be asked to send along part of or all of the manuscript.

3. If your book is accepted, sign with a reputable publishing house. If the publishing house is impressed by your work, you will be given an offer. Look at your contract carefully and sign it if it meets your demands.

4. Revise with an editor. Work with an editor to revise your book until it is ready for publication.

5. Market your book. While you're waiting for the book to be released, market the book to everyone you know — and people you don't know. Once your book is published, you will have to continue to advertise for your book. You can enjoy your publication, but remember that marketing should never stop. Promote your book through blogging, interviewing, and reading from your book. Develop a Facebook fan page and website to advertise your book.

Self Publish Your Book

1. Look up self-publishing companies.

2. Create an account with the company that works for you.

3. Write your book on Microsoft Word or other programs like that. Most self-publishing companies will re□uire you to upload a Microsoft Word file of your book.

4. Choose the size and type of book you would like (paperback vs. hardcover).

5. After completing the steps it takes to self-publish your book, make it available for people to purchase it. Make sure to provide a choice of a payment method so you can receive the money you earn from each book sold.

6. Advertise your book. Begin by telling friends and family. This will increase your chances of having your books purchased by others. Use social media and online advertising to get your book known even further.

CHAPTER 7: 10 SIMPLE STEPS TO SELF-PUBLISH

1. Choose a topic.

This is often the hardest part for writers — "What the heck do I write about?"

Let's talk about non-fiction writing for moment. Grab a pen and paper and start writing down all of your skills (personal and professional), your interests, your hobbies, any significant life challenges you've faced, and any other knowledge you've gained as part of living.

Write down every possible thing you can think of until you've exhausted your brain. Now go back through that list and pick 3-4 topics that you would actually enjoy writing about. If you hate the topic, writing will be drudgery.

Once you have a few possible topics, break those down into possible sub-topics. For example, if you have an interest in sewing, sub-topics might include how to sew curtains or hand stitching.

You want your topic to be broad enough that you could write a series of books about various elements of it. It's better to go deep into one aspect of a subject than to try to cover everything in one book.

This gives you the opportunity to build a catalog of books, and it gives your reader more bang for the buck with each book you write.

After you've selected a few topics, you'll need to do some research to see if the topic is viable and has enough interested readers to make it profitable for you.

2. Write your book.

Let me tell you upfront — you don't have to be an extraordinary writer to write a good book. You just need to be good enough to communicate what you have to say in a clear, concise, and interesting way.

Write a "crappy first draft." In other words, just get it down on paper and then go back and refine it. So with complete permission to write a crappy first draft, you can get started with these steps:

Decide how much time you can devote to writing each day. Even if it's just 5 minutes, carve that time out as sacred writing time. Don't allow anything or anyone to disturb or distract you.

Write an outline first. Break your topic down into possible chapters or sections, and then bullet point the info that will fit into each of them.

Sit down and write for your allotted time. Just write even if you aren't happy with it. Write in a conversational way so your authentic voice comes through.

Increase your writing time or word count over time. If you want to get more done, set increasingly bigger goals for yourself.
 For example, you might have a goal to write 500-1000 words a day. You could finish a 30,000 word non-fiction book in a month or two. For reference, I've written almost 1000 words to this point in my post.

3. Edit your book.
We strongly recommend you get an editor to go through your book before you publish. Even if you're the most amazing writer in the world, you still need an editor. You need someone to polish your work, make sure it flows, and catch any mistakes. Please don't skip this step. It's that important.

Of course you'll want to edit your own book several times before you send it to an editor. Go through it with a fine-tooth comb and re-write and edit carefully. You might even ask someone who's your ideal reader to look at your manuscript before you send it to an editor.

For example, if you're writing a book on parenting teenagers, find someone you know who is the parent of a teenager and ask them to read your draft. Ask for honest feedback so you can make sure the book appeals to the audience you're trying to reach.

Try to have a thick skin when getting this feedback and see it as an opportunity to make your book the best it can be.

Once you feel the book is ready for the editor's finishing touches, start looking for a good editor. You can find them at places like Upwork, ArchangelInk, and Elance. Interview a few people and look at some of the books they've edited, particularly in your niche. Many editors can also format your book for publishing on Kindle and for print.

4. Decide on a title.
There's a real art and science to choosing a good title for your book. You want a title that has a "hook" — something short and pithy that really grabs the reader's attention. The subtitle can be longer with more explanation about how the book benefits the reader.

Go on Amazon and look at some of the bestsellers in your niche. Examine the titles and pay attention to those that really jump out at you. You'll also want to consider some of the SEO keywords in your niche that could be included in your title or subtitle to help readers find your book.

I like to write several title ideas and then run them by my blog readers and social media followers. If you don't have a blog or social media following, you can use a service like Pick FU to have a sampling of people weigh in on your titles.

Try to get a lot of feedback from potential readers to see what resonates with them before you settle on a title that you like. We talk more about how to select your book title in our free video series.

5. Design your book cover.
This is another area of self-publishing where you should hire a pro. Please . . . don't choose a cheesy stock photo and slap up your title just because it's the cheapest way to go. Find someone who regularly designs book covers and pay to have your cover well-designed.

I promise this step will pay off in the long run, as more people will be inclined to buy a book with an eye-catching, great looking cover. You can also find cover designers at ArchangelInk, Elance, and Upwork, so go through the same vetting process you used to hire your editor.

Look at their past work, ask about deadlines, and find out how many revisions are included in the price estimate.

You will need to write copy for the back cover of a print version of your book. This copy should focus on the benefits of your book for the reader. Give them a compelling reason why they must have your book.

You only have a little space on the back cover, so be concise and use language that invites the reader to learn more. You can also include a very brief bio and photo of yourself, as well as a testimonial or review praising your book if you want.

6. Format your book.
I hire someone to format my books for me. Formatting for both Kindle and CreateSpace (Amazon's print on demand service for print books) is time-consuming and tedious. So unless you just love detail work, try to find an editor who will also handle formatting your book for you.
Another reason to hire someone is that you want to be sure it's done correctly. You don't want to go to all of the trouble to write your book, only to have it look like a mess

when someone opens it to read it. Find someone who does this for a living and knows all of the rules and requirements of proper formatting.

7. Upload your book to Kindle.
Once your book is edited and formatted, and you have the cover designed, you can upload your book on the Kindle store. You'll need to create an account with Kindle Direct Publishing (KDP), where you'll find all the instructions for uploading your book, creating an author page, setting pricing for your book, and writing copy for your sales page.

All of these steps are really important when it comes to getting your book noticed and selling a lot of copies. The copy for your author page and your book sales page should focus primarily on how your book benefits the reader.

You don't need to sell people on the features of the book or what a great author you are. You need to let them know how you can answer their questions, offer solutions to their problems, and help them overcome their challenges related to your topic.

Once you've uploaded the book and completed the author page and sales page, it's time to hit the publish button. It generally takes Amazon a few days to review your book and make it live, but once they do, you are officially a published author!

8. Publish your print book.
I use CreateSpace, Amazon's print on-demand service, to create the print version of my books, although there are many other places to print your book. If you've hired someone to format your book for you, be sure you ask them to format for both Kindle and CreateSpace (or whatever printing service you use).

Once your book is formatted for print, and your cover designs (front, back and spine) are completed, you can upload all of the files on CreateSpace by following their set-up instructions. CreateSpace has a help center and comprehensive book services (formatting, editing, and design) if you run into any problems.

Once you have everything properly uploaded, you can send your book to Amazon for publishing at the click of a button.

9. Promote your book.
So now that your book is published, you'll be waiting for the cash to start rolling in, right? Well, don't rely on Amazon alone to promote your book. You will need to spread the word and do everything you can to market and promote your book.

If you have a blog, be sure to write about your book and how it will help your readers. If you have an email list, be sure you send out an email announcing your new book. Use social media as well to spread the word.
You might also consider writing guest posts on relevant blogs about your topic with a link to your author page in the bio of the guest post. You can offer your books through various other publishing channels, like Nook and Kobo, if you don't want to just rely on Amazon. Keep marketing your book regularly so it doesn't get lost in obscurity.

10. Start writing your next book.
The best way to become a better writer and to sell more books is by writing more books. Think about creating a catalog of books around your topic, so people interested in your topic will be more inclined to by from you.
The more books you write, the more income your books will bring you monthly.
Always have a book in process, and you'll discover with a regular writing habit, you can publish several books a year.

CHAPTER 8: PRINT ON DEMAND BOOKS

Before you dive headlong into creating a paperback version of your ebook you should ask yourself why you want a print version in the first place, which will give you all the information you need to choose the right print partner to achieve your self-publishing goals.

Many of the decisions regarding printing your books will depend on your goals. If you only intend to sell online, you'll have fewer decisions to make. If you intend to try and get into brick-and-mortar stores, you have a lot more to consider. Quality and cost are considerations, but ease of use also comes into play when making your POD decisions.

On demand printing is the biggest revolution in book printing since the Gutenberg press, making it convenient and affordable for self-published authors to print and sell their books straight to readers around the world.

In the past, self-published authors were plagued with large upfront costs, printing more books than necessary, and managing excess inventory on their own. **Print On Demand** erases those troubles with an efficient small-run printing process that still provides maximum exposure, but with more author control and minimal investment.

If this kind of self publishing is for you, then a print-on-demand publisher is exactly what you're looking for. You don't need to spend much (or any) money upfront – all you really do is publicise your book and the buyers can get one made when they want it. Meanwhile, you could be making a small amount or a large amount in passive income and it hasn't cost you much except your time spent writing. Sounds good?

Choosing your print-on-demand (POD) book publisher is another thing entirely. In the end, it comes down to your needs and your particular book. For instance, some publishers are better at printing novels or photography books than others. Some will give you better royalties, while others will do a better job of helping you with promotion.

Determine your POD goals

Choosing a print partner is not as much about money as it might seem at first. It's a decision that can only be answered after you determine exactly what you want to do with your printed book. Here are five questions to ask yourself:

-Are you going to be primarily an ebook author with a few printed books for promotional purposes?
-Are you going to restrict print sales to online, through the pbook retailer and your own website?
-Are you going to limit yourself to a few local or handpicked bookstores?
-Are you going to go all out and try to get a distributor and do a print campaign with the associated trade-style publicity in newspapers and other media that is necessary to sell books in this way. If yes, why?
-Have you realistically budgeted time and money costs?

Four of The Best Online Print-On-Demand Book Publishers

1. Blurb

Blurb is well known for its full colour photography-based books, however it also offers a couple of black and white text novel options. You can either use their online software to prepare a book or you can upload a pre-prepared PDF. Whichever option you choose, there's no upfront costs.
When you sell the book, Blurb takes a small fee. Plus, you can set your own prices and thereby choose your own profit margin. Blurb offers payments through PayPal.

2. Lulu

Lulu is one of the larger publishers and will happily cater for many types of books. You can easily publish a novel, a cookbook, or simply create a photo book for your family. They have the ability to publish and sell eBooks on your behalf and claim to have the largest distribution channels of all online publishers. Useful free services include consultations, while paid services offered include cover design, ISBN purchasing and distribution. If you choose to sell in the Lulu Marketplace without an ISBN, your upfront costs are negligible.

You can also set your profits by choosing your own royalties and Lulu makes its money by taking a small cut from your sales. Lulu pays royalties via Paypal or cheque. Read more about publishing with Lulu here.

3. Wordclay

Wordclay offers a basic DIY publishing service which is free for publishers. If you wish to pay a modest fee, services such as editing, ISBNs and distribution are available to you as well.

Again, you can choose your own royalty and Wordclay takes a cut from your sales. Wordclay sends US cheques.

4. CreateSpace (aka Booksurge)

CreateSpace offers a DIY "no fees upfront" royalty-based publishing option to complement their regular publishing offers. They are actually part of the Amazon group of companies, so there's no extra fees involved to distribute your book through Amazon. ISBNs can be obtained for free via CreateSpace.

CreateSpace also claimS to offer the best royalties in the business "" plus they allow you to choose your own royalty. Royalties can be paid by US cheque or to a US bank account.

Word of Advice

When choosing your publisher, make sure you research well and ensure it's a good fit for you before you commit your time and money or sign any agreements. Companies such as these do have the occasional unhappy customer but it's not the norm. Here's a few important things to look out for:

For non-US citizens, remember that different companies have different tax witholding requirements and that the cheque fees and your ability to deposit US cheques may devalue your earnings somewhat.

Having your book formally listed with an ISBN will often require you to ensure the quality of your book. This may require you to purchase a copy of your book each and every time you make a change (this can include price or directory changes). If you sign up for an ISBN, read the fine print, be prepared to purchase if required and don't make changes to your book after this unless it's very important.

No-frills DIY publishers will endeavour to make money from added extras such as cover art, editing and ISBNs. If you want to use these services, ensure you compare the prices between publishers and the cost of doing it yourself.

Bonus Chapter: Expand Your Product Distribution and Make More Money Without Any Added Cost.

CHAPTER 9: AUDIOBOOK CREATION EXCHANGE (ACX)

Maximizing your time and effort is the name of the game here and that's exactly the point of turning your book into an audio version. It also exposes your brand to a whole new audience being that not everyone has the ability to read and some people may just prefer to listen to a book as opposed to reading one. Whatever the reason, creating an audio version of your book will be beneficial to both you and your audience.

The kicker to creating an audiobook in ACX is that your book will not only be available on Amazon, it will be available on Audible.com and Itunes. We all know that these big name websites generate millions of views on a daily basis, this means your book will be exposed to millions of buyers on rotation. You really can't beat that free promotion and to put the icing on the cake...it's totally free to sign up!

You are considered to be a rights holder to your book so you would watch this short video to get signed up quickly on the ACX platform. Some authors may opt to narrate their own books and others may want someone more seasoned in that area to narrate for them. It all depends on your personal preference. However, if you would like to find a narrator, ACX makes this easy to do. Simply post a short sample of your book to act as an audition piece for the potential narrator. You have the option to post your book so people can audition or listen to some narration samples and choose who you want to audition for the role.

Once you select your narrator, ACX makes it easy for you to make this narrator an offer by sending them a done-for-you offer letter or "production offer page." Once a deal is made your narrator gets to work on your book. At this point ACX initiates a 15 minute checkpoint for your narrator to record and upload the narration to the platform for approval from you. This checkpoint is imposed in order to assure that you and the narrator are on one accord in regards to the direction of the book. Once approved, the narrator has the ability to narrate the entire book.

You are alotted 2 rounds of revisions to your book and once satisfied, you pay your narrator unless you agreed to the royalty offer that ACX has in place. From this point your audio book gets distributed to the Amazon, Audio.com, and Itune platforms. It's very important to decide on whether you are granting ACX exclusive rights to your book or non-exclusive because giving sole rights away greatly limits your ability to distribute your book to other platforms, which in turn, stagnates opportunities for additional income gain.

Of course, adequate promotion of your audiobook through means of social media, blogs, forums, and websites are essential to the success of your work. ACX issues monthly payments via royalty statements and direct deposit. In order to learn more about this valuable tool and how to take your book to the next level, visit here.

CONCLUSION

With the change of times and swift developments in technology, becoming a published author has never been so accessible. Being that the culture today is one that is more about getting things done on demand and the motto is, "right now," the days of traditional publishing are fading fast. Self-publishing has come along and is kicking butt in taking over the writing industry. This type of publishing has endless benefits that gives the author more creative control over how their book is created, distributed, marketed, and viewed by the masses.

Platforms such as Amazon, Kindle Direct Publishing, and CreateSpace have given authors the ability and assistance to become a more independent entity. These platforms have breathed life into the work of authors who would otherwise never be discovered due to the costs and lengthy time spans of traditional publishing. With these platforms becoming a published author is as easy as literally clicking a button on your laptop.

Of course, there are basic things that a writer needs to know how to do before even presenting their work to the self-publishing platforms. There is a need to have spelling, grammar, and syntax knowledge. Your book should also have a clear goal and objective because a purpose is always a great thing to have when writing. Before you can self-publish, your book has to be in a certain format that should be laid out in the directives of each platform that you plan on using. There are many author's out there who ignore the basics, throw anything out there, and slap their name on it. This isn't going to fly if you are serious about becoming a well-established, authoritative author.

The best way to gain authority and gain trust as an author would be to **create a fan base** (YouTube, blogs, podcast), create actionable content, write books, get published. This method has been used repetitively by authors who have gone on to sell billions and it all started with an idea, a pen, and the notion to self-publish.

www.ingramcontent.com/pod-product-compliance
Lightning Source LLC
Chambersburg PA
CBHW050024230526
45470CB00003B/1121